MW01093913

Subway Circus

by William Saroyan

SAMUEL FRENCH

FOUNDED 1830

New York Hollywood London Toronto

SAMUELFRENCH.COM

SUBWAY CIRCUS

PREFACE

I was in New York in May, 1935. One day *The New York Times* said I had written a play or was going to write one. I had bought a ticket to Europe. The boat was sailing in five days. I had *not* written a play. But it seemed to me that there was enough time before the sailing of the boat to write one. Nobody wants to make a liar of *The New York Times*. Before the boat sailed, Subway Circus was written. Once again *The New York Times* had printed news fit to print. I called Subway Circus a play. It is probably no such thing. It is very likely a theatrical entertainment of some sort.

Subway Circus is the first work for the theatre I wrote after becoming a published writer. No producer wanted it. Inasmuch as I knew my work in the theatre would be unlike the work of other playwrights, and inasmuch as producers had no use for my first effort, I decided to forget the theatre for a time and continue writing in the short story form.

Subway Circus is composed of ten parts. Any who may wish to undertake a production of Subway Circus should feel free to choose from these parts, and to perform only those parts which they care to perform.

The playing of the whole work, or the playing of

selected parts of it, should be without intermission, and if possible without breaks. The sound of the traveling subway train will probably serve best to hold the various parts together, and keep the mood of the work unbroken. A true production of Subway Circus would have to be either a labor of love or an expensive gamble. I am not sure the work is worthy of either. Certain parts are pure ballet, certain other parts pure theatre. The last part is no more than the singing of a song. The work could be produced as a ballet, no doubt. And, on the other hand, it could also be produced as a play. Good dancers are seldom good actors, and vice versa, but the truth of the matter is Subway Circus should combine the several elements which are inherent in all entertainment. A good production of the whole work, while difficult, is not impossible.

The importance of Subway Circus is most probably that it indicates a direction, rather than reaches a destination. Group reading and rehearsing of parts of it, without sets, props, or sound effects, should be good practice for students of the theatre.

San Francisco
May 11, 1940.

SUBWAY CIRCUS

NOTE

Here is the world of one man at a time: the inner, the boundless, the ungeographical world of wakeful dream.

The object is to explore this world. To give substance and motion to some of its thought and mood.

The basic scene is a portion of the inside of a subway train.

The basic sound is the sound of the subway moving at various rates of speed, and stopping.

The passengers are very much like the passengers of any subway train. Each time the train stops, some of the passengers get off, and others get on.

In the meantime, the dreams of some of the passengers are materialized.

The theatrical method is this:

A light falls upon the person whose dream is to be revealed. The subway train divides in the middle, in darkness, and the place of this person's dream is revealed. The dream unfolds while the sound of the moving subway continues.

The play begins with the subway and ends with the subway. Begins and ends with the real world. The beginning and end of each dream is the subway: except for the subway and these dreamers aboard, these dreams could not be.

There is a sense of hurry in each episode: a sense of rushing to catch the train. The dreamer, in dream, and in the dream-place, hurries to the turnstile, drops a nickel very loudly, the place of the dream vanishes in darkness, and the subway train reappears with its passengers, including the dreamer.

SUBWAY CIRCUS

1

QUESTIONS AND ANSWERS

SUBWAY CIRCUS

1

The Dreamer: A small BOY.

Others: A TEACHER. *The* PRINCIPAL *of the School.*

THE SCENE: *A back-drop on which is painted a warm sun, a clean simple landscape of brown earth, one green tree, one flying bird, one brook, one cloud, one skyscraper.*

Three grammar-school desks. Blackboard. Map.

The BOY *comes sullenly to his desk, seeming to be talking to himself. The* TEACHER *is a young girl. The* PRINCIPAL *is an old man who is dozing in a chair.*

THE TEACHER. Now, John, if a farmer has seven apples, and he gives away three apples, how many apples remain?

THE BOY. What kind of apples?

THE TEACHER. Any kind. Now, if the farmer has seven, and gives away three, how many remain?

THE BOY. What color are the apples? Who is the farmer?

THE TEACHER. I will have to punish you if you refuse to answer my question. This is a problem of arithmetic.

THE BOY. I want to know about the farmer. Where does he live?

(The TEACHER *takes the* BOY *by the ear to the* OLD MAN.)

THE BOY. Who is the farmer? What color are the apples?

THE TEACHER. Mr. Smith, this boy will not answer my question.

THE PRINCIPAL. What *is* the question, Mary?

THE TEACHER. If a farmer has seven apples, and he gives away three apples, how many apples remain?

THE PRINCIPAL. What kind of apples, Mary?

THE TEACHER. Why, it doesn't say what kind, Mr. Smith. It says seven apples, and gives away three.

THE PRINCIPAL. Who is the farmer, Mary? I never heard of a farmer who would give away three apples.

THE TEACHER. I don't know.

THE PRINCIPAL. Well, Mary, you can hardly blame the boy for wanting to know who the farmer is. Are the apples wormy?

THE TEACHER. I don't know, Mr. Smith. But the answer is four.

THE PRINCIPAL. I hardly agree, Mary.

THE TEACHER. Well, how many, then?

THE PRINCIPAL. It's not a question of how many. My God, what's the world coming to? Here, boy, you ask the teacher a question. *(He goes away.)*

There is a moment of silence. The subway itself is silent. Then it begins to rattle again.

The BOY *tries to speak but can't. His voice is heard as a whisper, greatly magnified, from the darkness, over a microphone.*

THE BOY'S VOICE. If you have seven, and you give away three: seven and three. Fifty-five, sixty: sixty-five, seventy: seventy-five, eighty: one thousand, two thousand, three thousand, four thousand, five, six, seven, eight, nine, ten. Zero, one, two: ten million, eleven million, twelve million, a billion minutes, hours, days. A farmer with a farm. A tree with apples. The farmer has seven, and he gives away. Three, four, five, six, seven.

While his thought is being articulated in this manner, a clock ticks loudly, the brightness of the sun increases, the subway roars, and he stands staring at the YOUNG GIRL, *who is supposed to teach him about the world, and living in it.*

When the whispering ends, the clock stops, and the subway quiets down.

THE BOY. I don't know what to ask. Can you tell me what is a street?

THE TEACHER. Nothing.

THE BOY. Can you tell me why everything in the world is many things?

THE TEACHER. *I don't know.*

THE BOY. Can you tell me why everything changes every minute and is always the same? Why the apples grow and rot and grow again and rot again and grow again, years and years of apples growing, people living, streets traveling around and around the world? *(The* TEACHER *gestures.)*

The Subway roars, the sun grows very dim. A light falls on the turnstile. The BOY *turns to go.*

THE BOY. Can you tell me why I'm alone when I have a mother, a father, brothers, sisters, and the whole world full of people? Can you tell me who I am?

*HE drops a nickel and passes beyond the turnstile.
The scene begins to fade.*

*Back to the subway train again. The BOY is seated
among the people, staring at everything.*

SUBWAY CIRCUS

2

MAN, THE ACROBAT

The Dreamer: A Cripple. *He is a small man with an immense deformed chest and short legs.*

The Scene: *A back-drop on which is painted an abstract city over which a trapeze swings and makes shadows. The city is full of large staring eyes. The stage is a dance floor.*

This is the event:

The Cripple *walks to the Center of the dance floor and in the dim light casts away his deformity, casting away his coat. He lifts himself out of his crooked body and stands tall and free. A slow sentimental waltz. A* Woman *walks to him from the darkness. They dance.*

The City *and* The World *stare and speak: one word: over a microphone: Look. Look. Look.*

The tempo of the music changes louder and swifter. The music ceases and the Lady *goes away. The light increases. The* Cripple *casts away all of his clothes.*

He is now an acrobat, one whose body is precise in time and motion.

The World *says: Look. Look.*

Still, the Cripple *is not pleased. He beckons to the sky and a trapeze falls.*

He swings on the trapeze.

He leaps to the stage, walks on his hands, tumbles.

He is showing the world, performing the body of man alive in time and space.

He returns to the trapeze: but now it will not swing, and he begins to lose his strength.

The World: *Look. Look.*

He sets the trapeze into motion, then leaps, off-stage, and falls.

Crash and confusion: subway: The World *saying: Look. Look.*

The stage is empty for a moment. The Cripple *returns to the Center of the stage. Again himself, a small man with an immense deformed chest.*

And back to the subway.

SUBWAY CIRCUS

3

THE LOVERS

The Dreamers: A STENOGRAPHER *and a* CLERK. *They are seated together in the subway.*

THE SCENE: *Portion of an office, with a desk and a typewriter. The back-drop is an empty movie screen.*

The Event:

The GIRL *is at the desk, typing. The* CLERK *brings her some papers, moving automatically, and goes away without even noticing her. The* GIRL *stares at the screen, sighs, and begins to type again. The* CLERK *returns with more papers and this time notices her. It is like a discovery. He is amazed, almost stunned. This beautiful girl, here. In the same place. He would like to speak to her, but cannot do so.*

Staring at her his feeling is articulated:

THE VOICE. Mary. I love you, Mary. I love you because you are here with me, because you are so small and sad, because you work so hard, because you want so much of fourteen dollars a week, because you are alone. Mary, I love you. Love me and I will rob a bank and buy you clothes and a big automobile for each of us, and we will drive to California together. Love me, Mary, and I will steal a million dollars and we will ride all over the world together. We will go to the warm countries, Mary, where melons grow and the sun is strong. Mary, we will walk in the sun together. We will run together, Mary. At the river we will take off our clothes and swim together.

THE GIRL. Well, what are you waiting for?

THE BOY. Nothing. *(He goes away.)*

The GIRL *begins to type again. The scene darkens and the empty screen fills with moving pictures of Clark Gable, Gary Cooper, Frederic March, Paul Muni, and a couple of others. Flashes of each, all silent, while the* GIRL *types and stares.*

THE GIRL. Ah. Ah. *(She stands, and begins walking around desk)* Oh, Clark. Oh, Gary. Oh, Frederick. Oh. Paul.

The pictures cease. The light increases. The GIRL *sits at her desk.*

The CLERK *returns. He stands over the* GIRL *timidly.*

His voice, loudly, while he looks down at her, wanting to touch her but not daring to do so:

THE VOICE. Don't cry. God Almighty, I love you. Please don't cry. I love you. Ah, baby, love me and I will steal money enough to buy you everything you want. Please don't cry. You're not alone any more, baby. I love you.

He touches her shoulder gently. The GIRL *leaps to her feet, frightened.*

THE GIRL. What do you want?

THE BOY. I.

THE GIRL. Oh, go away.

THE BOY. Mr. Smith said to get these letters out tonight.

THE GIRL. Well, all right, but go away. Why are you staying here?

THE BOY. I want to marry you.

THE GIRL. What?

THE BOY. Yes.

THE GIRL. Oh, go away.

THE BOY. I can afford it. I got a raise last week. I get twenty a week now.

THE GIRL. Don't make me laugh.

THE BOY. I guess we could manage.

THE GIRL. You're crazy.

THE BOY. I love you. Mary, I love you.

THE GIRL. We've been working in this office three years together. What's eating *you* all of a sudden?

THE BOY. I just like you, that's all.

THE GIRL. I got work to do. Leave me alone.

THE BOY. I'm nobody, but I love you, Mary. I could live without you all right, but honest, Mary, I don't *want* to live without you.

THE GIRL. Leave me alone. I don't like you. I hate you. Even to be near you makes me sick. We've been working together in this office three years. I hate this place. I hate everything and everybody in this place.

THE BOY. Mary, I'll take you away. I'll take you to California.

THE GIRL. What?

THE BOY. Yes. I'll steal. I'll rob a bank. I'll get a million dollars of the money, and we'll ride to California. You in a Cadillac, and me in a Packard. I love you.

THE GIRL. Leave me alone.

THE BOY. What good is California without you? What good is anything? I need you. (*He tries to embrace the* GIRL) I'm afraid. I've got sixty dollars in the bank and I'm afraid I'll do something crazy. What the hell are we doing *here?* We're here in the

Spring and in the Summer and in the Fall and in the Winter, and outside is the whole blooming world. Why do we have to stay here when there are so many other places?

THE GIRL. I'll love you. We won't get married. I don't want to be anybody's wife. We'll go to a hotel tonight. *(She stares at the empty screen.)*

And back to the subway.

SUBWAY CIRCUS

4

THE HERO

4

The Dreamer: A small, ineffectual MAN.

Others: A BIG MAN. *A* FAT LADY. *A* POLICEMAN.
One half dozen UNITED STATES MARINES.

THE SCENE: *A back-drop on which is painted a*
large picture of someone like Lionel Strongfort:
also headlines from Strongfort's advertisements,
such as: BE A MAN: CLIP THE COUPON:
also appropriate pictures of ladies in tights
from the "Police Gazette."

The Event:

The SMALL MAN *is shoved around in the subway*
by the BIG MAN *and the* FAT LADY *who reap-*
pear in the dream.

There is one half of a prize-fight ring on the stage,
with ropes.

The SMALL MAN *appears, strutting. He shadow*
boxes.

The BIG MAN *appears, timidly.*

THE SMALL MAN. Come here. *(The* BIG MAN
does, of course.) Remember me?

He floors the BIG MAN *with one fantastic swipe and continues to strut around, waving his arms.*

Music, and a cry of: Wow.

The FAT LADY *appears.*

HE *floors the* LADY *with an even more fantastic swipe, and then the pace swiftens.*

The POLICEMAN *appears, blowing a whistle. The* SMALL MAN *floors the* POLICEMAN.

A drum rolls. The music is military. SIX MARINES *arrive.*

One by one and with the greatest of ease the SMALL MAN *floors each of the* MARINES.

There is applause and cheering.

And back to the subway. The subway stops, the door opens, and the SMALL MAN *makes his exit. Very sheepishly, with a shove from the* FAT LADY.

SUBWAY CIRCUS

5

THE JEW IN THE WORLD

5

*The Dreamer: An old JEW with a Biblical beard.
He is reading a Yiddish newspaper.*

*Others: A small JEWISH BOY of nine or ten, and
his SISTER, several years older.*

The event is this:

The old JEW speaks in Yiddish to these children.

The idea is this:

*Through the dignity of his speech, to capture the
passion and fortitude of the Jew in the world.*

*And the tragic humor. During his speech, he laughs.
It is hearty laughter, but it is heavy with grief.*

*The scene is this: A portion of a synagogue. Burn-
ing candles. On the back-drop is painted a vast
and angry head of Moses, and a world with
closed doors.*

*The entire spisode is accompanied by Jewish mu-
sic. There is singing, sometimes a male and a
female voice together, sometimes a chorus of
voices. The music varies as the mood of the OLD
MAN varies.*

29

The CHILDREN *kiss his hand.*

The old and the new. The wisdom and experience and fortitude of the old. The eagerness and innocence of the young.

The OLD MAN *speaks with rage and fury. The* CHILDREN *cling to him.*

There is a sound of multitudes walking.

The sound of many people walking begins with only one person walking, then two, then three, and so on until it is a multitude; with Jewish music.

And back to the subway.

SUBWAY CIRCUS

6

THE SOCIAL REVOLUTION

6

The Dreamer: A LADY *of forty or so: poor: and
socially ambitious. She is reading "Vogue."*

*Others: A small crowd of the inane and garrulous,
male and female, etcetera. A lousy* WRITER. *A
lousy* PAINTER. *A lousy* PIANIST. *A bogus*
COUNT. *And maybe a couple of others. In short,
the best people.*

THE SCENE: *A back-drop on which is painted one
inane king (long live the king), one inane queen
(long live the queen), one handsomely outfitted
troop of soldiers (long live the soldiers), one
impossible coat of arms, one winking eye (the
eye winks appropriately during the events of this
episode), one high-tone dwelling, one fancy
street, one classy carriage with horses.*

*The stage is a drawing room: a few pieces of furni-
ture, a table with bottles and glasses, a piano, a
radio, etcetera.*

The event:

This poor LADY *is* NOT *a poor lady. She is a society
dame: a lady who entertains the rich and im-
portant, all tired and weary. She is dressed to
kill, God love her. She is the well-known Mrs.*

33

Smith whose picture appears so often in the society pages of newspapers.

So she entertains.

The smart people arrive one at a time. Each is announced by a big BUTLER *who has a strong voice. After each announcement a loud Bronx cheer is heard. And the eye winks. Every man is named Smith. The first name is always John. Every lady is named Smith. The first name is Mary. The men kiss the* LADY'S *hand. As a rule. The ladies embrace her. As a rule. The Bronx cheer is heard after every performance of one or another of these charming formalities.*

A number of the guests have already arrived when the episode begins.
They are talking swiftly, holding glasses. Throughout the episode they talk. They say anything and everything and they say everything in the same way, so that NONE *of it means anything. I'm not going to put down their actual words because it isn't worth it. They talk about literature, painting, sculpture, music, drama, government, religion, writers, poets, painters, sculptors, composers, actors, actresses, movies, politicians, private experiences, and sometimes they even mention the weather. Nothing they say is intelligible, although some words are.*

THE BUTLER. *(I guess they call them butlers. I'm not sure. Anyway, he's the guy who is nobody and knows it and is proud of it and sometimes puts a little humor and satire into his announcements of the guests)* Mr. John Smith. *(A hearty Bronx cheer. A wink.)* This Mr. Smith is the writer. You can tell he is a lousy writer by the way he smiles at everybody. *(He doesn't kiss the lady's hand.)*

THE LADY. Oh, I am so glad to see you again. How did you find Paris? Isn't Paris too lovely?

THE WRITER. It was charming. Charming.

THE LADY. I'm always sad when I'm away from Paris.

(A hearty Bronx cheer. A wink. A FLUNKEY brings a tray with drinks. The WRITER takes one without looking at the FLUNKEY.)

THE BUTLER. Mr. John Smith. *(A hearty Bronx cheer. A wink.)* This Mr. Smith is a painter. What the hell. Who cares what he is? He is a genius.

(The PAINTER stoops gallantly and kisses the LADY'S hand: Bronx cheer. Wink.)

THE LADY. Oh, I am so glad to see you again. How did you find London? Isn't London too divine?

THE PAINTER. It was charming. Charming. The fog, you know?

THE LADY. Yes, yes, the fog. How I miss the London fog. I'm always miserable when I'm away from London.

(Drinks etcetera for the great PAINTER. He joins the loiterers and one more voice is added to the chorus.)

THE BUTLER. Mr. John Smith. *(A hearty Bronx cheer. A wink.)* Miss Mary Smith. This one is a debutante. She is beautiful beyond repair. I got that from vaudeville.

(The DEBUTANTE and the LADY embrace: a couple of Bronx cheers. Two winks.)

THE LADY. Oh, I am so glad to see you again, my dear. How did you find Vienna?

THE DEBUTANTE. Vienna? Vienna? Oh, I shall never be happy again till I return to Vienna.

THE LADY. I am always homesick when I am away from Vienna.

THE BUTLER. Miss Mary Smith. This Miss Smith was very young shortly after the Boer War. The War and passing years aged her swiftly.

(A hearty Bronx cheer. A wink. The ELDERLY MISS SMITH embraces the LADY.)

THE LADY. Oh, I am so glad to see you again, darling. How did you find Naples?

THE ELDERLY MISS SMITH. It stank. It simply stank, my dear.

THE LADY. Yes, yes, how Naples stinks. And how does it feel to be home again?

THE ELDERLY MISS SMITH. Lousy. It feels lousy, simply lousy.

THE LADY. Yes, I know. Lousy, simply lousy.

(Drinks etcetera and another voice etcetera, but not a bad one.)

THE BUTLER. Mr. John Smith. *(A hearty Bronx cheer. A wink.)* This punk plays the piano.

(The LADY asks him how he found Berlin and he says he found Berlin fascinating. Then he begins to play the piano.)

THE BUTLER. *(To the LADY)* All the guests have arrived, Madam. I guess the bogus Count arrived earlier in the evening, through a window.

THE LADY. Very good, John. You may stand by the door and watch. Please try to seem delighted.

THE BUTLER. *(A wit)* I am delighted, Madam. Look. *(He makes a delighted face.)* See?

(The BUTLER *stands by the door. A* FLUNKEY *passes. The fine people are going at top speed. The* FLUNKEY *hands the* BUTLER *a pamphlet.)*

THE BUTLER. *(Reading)* Communist Manifesto. Karl Marx. Dialectical materialism. Revolution. Brotherhood on earth. Imperialist war. Imperialist baloney. What the hell. *(He throws the pamphlet away.)*

(The people are going strong. The best people, I mean. The FLUNKEY *returns with a tray of drinks.)*

THE FLUNKEY. *(Intimately to the* BUTLER*)* Comrade, the time is ripe for the revolution. Soon we shall be the kings and they shall be the slaves.

(A hearty Bronx cheer. A wink.)

THE BUTLER. Take it easy or you'll drop that tray.
THE FLUNKEY. Comrade, you are a jackass. You are ignorant. You do not know what is going on in the world. They are fat with eating while we starve. They ride around in Packards while we walk and hitch-hike. They go to five-dollar operas while we go to ten-cent movies. They—

(He drops the tray. Smash. Silence. The fine people stare at the rebel, stunned, amazed, horrified. A scream or two: Traitor, traitor.)

THE FLUNKEY. All right, look at me. Take a good look at me. I am nobody. I am a slave. Well, I'll show you. *(He brings a red flag from his pocket and waves it. MUSIC: "The Internationale."*) I am Russia, do you hear? I am the new order in the world.

(A hearty Bronx cheer. Wink. The good people make swift exits and swift comments and exclamations. The room is empty except for the great dame.)

THE LADY. All is lost. My world crumbles.

(A Bronx cheer. Wink. And back to the subway.)

SUBWAY CIRCUS

7

AFRICA-HARLEM EXPRESS

7

The Dreamers: A slim young NEGRESS, *and a dapper young* NEGRO.

THE SCENE: *On one half of the back-drop is painted a jungle and the word "Africa," and on the other half is painted a street and several buildings and the word "Harlem."*

On the stage, in front of the African side of the back-drop is one tree, and on the Harlem side is one lamp-post.

The Event:

From Africa to Harlem.

By the tree is the NEGRESS, *slim and very nearly naked. The light is dim.*

By the lamp-post is the NEGRO, *dapper and smart in fancy clothes.*

The NEGRESS *laughs.*

MALE. Who you, sister?
FEMALE. Ah'm Mary, colored boy. Who you?
MALE. Ah'm John Smith, sister. *In person.*

(They begin to move slowly, with rhythm.)

FEMALE. What you doin' heah, black boy?

MALE. Sister, dis is mah world. Ah live heah. De whole creation is mah world.

FEMALE. You look mighty like a stranger to me. I never see a man all covered up like you. Where's your shame? Who you hidin' from?

MALE. Sister, Ah ain't hidin'. Dese clothes are fo' decoration purposes.

FEMALE. Decoration purposes? I guess God done decorated every man enough. You got all de decoration you need under dem clothes. Why you hidin', black boy? You 'fraid of eyes?

MALE. Ah ain't 'fraid of nothin', sister. Ah'm just well-dressed. You is naked.

FEMALE. Naked? You crazy, man. Is de tree naked? Is de sky naked? Is de tiger naked? Ah got God's coverin', boy. Ah ain't ashamed.

(They begin to move faster, more rhythmically. There is a simple theme of music, quietly, mostly percussion.)

MALE. You come with me, sister, and Ah'll show you real class. Ah'll show you clothes. Dat's what. Hard leather fo' your feet and soft leather fo' your hands. Feathers fo' your head and silk fo' your body.

FEMALE. If Ah go, colored boy, where is dis place?

MALE. America is de place, sister.

FEMALE. Where dat, black boy?

MALE. You'll see.

FEMALE. Ah guess Ah want to see.

(The BOY takes the GIRL's hand and they do a sort of Cake Walk and leave the stage. The back-drop rises, revealing another depth of the stage and another back-drop. On this back-drop is painted a Southern landscape. Simple cabin. Magnolia

*tree. Rows of cotton. Lots of dark earth. Lots of
dark sky. The scene is a picture of a mood:
strength and sullenness. The* BOY *and* GIRL *re-
appear, each carrying a sack containing cotton.
The* GIRL *is wearing a cotton dress.)*

FEMALE. Is dis America, black boy?
MALE. *(Weary)* Dis is it, sister. Hold on, honey.
Hold on.
FEMALE. Ah's tired. All we do heah is work. From
de dark of mornin' to de dark of night. We is so
weary we can't dance or sing or look at de world.
CHORUS.
All the world is sad and weary everywhere I go.

*They leave the stage. The second back-drop rises and
a third is seen. On this back-drop is painted one
Harlem orchestra: instruments in groups of
three: especially trombones. Big drum. One
Chorus of black girls in feathers. Many colored
types in rows, forming an audience. The* BOY
and GIRL *appear again. The* GIRL *is almost
naked again, except for a few feathers here and
there. The* BOY *is dapper again. Hot music, and
the subway roar.*

They dance until they are almost exhausted.

FEMALE. Ah doan like it heah, black boy. Ah's
homesick. Ah'm goin' to my house and sleep. Ah
want to dream. Ah'm tired of noise. Ah'm weary of
dancin'. Ah remember a place of trees and warm
earth. Ah remember de clean sky and de cool water.
Ah'm goin' home.
MALE. You is just tired, dat's all. Ah'll take you
home, honey.

And back to the subway.

SUBWAY CIRCUS

8

THE MULTI-MILLIONAIRE

The Dreamer. A YOUNG MAN. *A fifteen-dollar-a-week clerk.*

Others: An ACCOUNTANT: *a man of fifty. A Postal Telegraph* MESSENGER BOY: *also fifty. A* MAN *selling whistles, harmonicas, etcetera: also fifty.*

THE SCENE: *On the back-drop is painted the board of the New York Stock Exchange. Wheat. Rye. Oats. Copper. Tin. Silver and: GOLD. One stock ticker around which is assembled a* CROWD OF PEOPLE, *male and female: Greed and fear. A picture of a bank: fine clean pillars. Calendars from 1929 to 1939.*

On the stage is one stock ticker which works about ten times as fast as a real stock ticker and makes about ten times as much noise. A desk, a chair, inside a railing.

The Event:

The fifteen-dollar-a-week CLERK *is rich. His feet are on the desk. He is smoking a cigar. A good cigar. He talks over a telephone: to ladies: to five tailors: to real estate agents: to automobile salesmen. He buys everything.*

THE ACCOUNTANT. *(Closing a book)* Your balance is now eighty-seven million dollars, sir.

THE CLERK. Call me John. I'm flesh and blood just like anybody else. Here. Take a look at this picture of me when I was three months old. God, what a change. How much did you say?

THE ACCOUNTANT. Eighty-seven million dollars.

THE CLERK. That's a lot of money. I guess that will last a long time.

THE ACCOUNTANT. Oh, no, sir. If the market begins to fall it won't last more than thirty minutes.

THE CLERK. Thirty minutes? *(He jumps over the railing.)* Then buy more real estate. Buy anything anybody offers for sale.

THE ACCOUNTANT. We've got two warehouses full of everything from toy machine-guns to real machine-guns already.

THE CLERK. Well, what land are you buying?

THE ACCOUNTANT. We practically own the State of Rhode Island.

THE CLERK. Rhode Island? That's a very small State. There's other land.

THE ACCOUNTANT. Yes, but worthless. There is a lot of worthless desert country in Texas. Forty-five cents an acre.

THE CLERK. How big is Texas?

THE ACCOUNTANT. Very big, sir. Larger than England, France, Germany, Italy, and Spain combined.

THE CLERK. Buy Texas. Don't delay. Make a long-distance telephone call immediately. Buy every inch of Texas.

THE ACCOUNTANT. The land is worthless, sir.

THE CLERK. You said desert, didn't you? The sun comes up over it, doesn't it? You can walk on it, can't you? Buy Texas. I want Texas. I want to go out there and walk on land I own.

(The MAN with the whistles and harmonicas appears. He blows one of those whistles that curl

up when you aren't blowing into them. This
makes a very pleasant note in music and a very
pleasant thing to see.)

THE CLERK. *(To the* PEDDLER*)* I haven't seen one
of those in years.

THE PEDDLER. Ten cents.

THE CLERK. Give me a dozen. What else you got?

THE PEDDLER. I got harmonicas, tin gazoos, oca-
rinoes, flutes, tambourines, castinets. Everything.

THE CLERK. You're just the man I've been looking
for. Where do they make these things?

THE PEDDLER. Some in Japan, some in Czecho-
Slovakia, some in Germany, some in America. I got
all kinds.

THE CLERK. All my life I've wanted a harmonica.
My name is John. I'm pleased to meet you. *(He
shakes hands with the* PEDDLER.*)*

THE PEDDLER. I play the harmonica like a bird. I
can play classical or jazz.

THE CLERK. Do you know *The Old Refrain?* My
mother used to sing that song to me. All my life I've
wanted to play *The Old Refrain* on the harmonica.

THE PEDDLER. Sure I can play it. *(He plays half
way through the song. Pauses:)* That was the jazz.
You like it?

THE CLERK. It's swell.

THE PEDDLER. I'll play it classical now. *(He plays.
The* CLERK *stands before him, amazed, smiling. A
violin joins the harmonica, and then an accordion.
Then a clear soprano singing the chorus.)*

THE CLERK. Do you think I could learn to play
like that?

THE PEDDLER. Sure. It's nothing. It's from the
heart. You don't have to know music. It's the same
as humming or whistling or singing.

THE CLERK. *(To the* ACCOUNTANT*)* Smith, give

this gentleman enough to pay for one dozen each of everything he's selling.

(The CLERK takes a harmonica and tries to play.)

THE ACCOUNTANT. *(To the PEDDLER)* How much is it? I'll write a check immediately.

THE PEDDLER. One dozen each is too many. I've got only two or three of each. One is enough. It is like humming, very simple. One is enough for a year.

THE ACCOUNTANT. You can get more, can't you?

THE PEDDLER. I can get thousands, but what for?

(The CLERK is trying to play the harmonica. The stock ticker begins to roll. It starts slowly and after a while it rolls very swiftly. The AC-COUNTANT runs to the ticker.)

THE ACCOUNTANT. *(To the PEDDLER)* Wait a few minutes, please. *(To the CLERK)* The market is fall-ing, sir.

THE CLERK. I'll figure this thing out some way. *He* can play it. I guess I can, too.

(The PEDDLER sits down. Every now and then he plays on one of the many things he has for sale: just killing time.)

THE CLERK. *(To the ACCOUNTANT)* By the way, Smith, get in touch with Mary Smith?

THE ACCOUNTANT. Mary Smith, sir? The siren of the cinema?

THE CLERK. Sure. I meant to tell you yesterday. Tell her I love her. How much do you think it's worth, confidentially?

THE ACCOUNTANT. I've never met the lady, sir. There are various fees, I understand.

THE CLERK. Start at twenty thousand dollars and go as high as fifty. If she won't accept, tell her I'll throw in three big cars, one yacht, three thoroughbred horses, and a private merry-go-round, if she cares for that sort of thing.

THE ACCOUNTANT. Yes, sir. But let me remind you, sir, that the market is falling. *(He points at the stock ticker and the* BOY *waves him away.)* Anything else, sir?

THE CLERK. No.

(The ACCOUNTANT *returns to the stock ticker. It is going strong. He is alarmed.)*

THE ACCOUNTANT. Mr. Smith, I am becoming a little alarmed about the market. It is falling very fast.

THE CLERK. Well, all right. Sell every share of stock I own.

THE ACCOUNTANT. We can't do that so easily, sir. The market won't be able to stand it. We'll cause a national panic.

THE CLERK. Go ahead and cause a national panic. All I want is my cash.

THE ACCOUNTANT. *(Telephoning)* Sell every share. Yes, yes. Every share. Immediately. And send over a statement of the balance immediately.

THE CLERK. Buy everything that can't come over a ticker.

THE ACCOUNTANT. The market's acting miserably, sir. I think we'd better wait till we get that statement.

THE CLERK. Is it really as bad as all that?

THE ACCOUNTANT. Yes, sir, I'm afraid so. ·It's pathetic, sir. It's fantastic. It's ridiculous. It's not right. Most shares are around three cents. Ten minutes ago they were selling around ninety-seven dollars. Looks as if something's happened.

THE CLERK. Three cents? God Almighty. *Smith!*

THE ACCOUNTANT. Yes, sir?

THE CLERK. Have you got any money on you?

THE ACCOUNTANT. I'm sorry, sir. I haven't a penny.

THE CLERK. God Almighty, neither have I. What's my balance, Smith? I've got to know.

THE ACCOUNTANT. I can't tell you, sir, until the statement arrives.

THE CLERK. I'd hate to go back to being a clerk at fifteen dollars a week.

THE ACCOUNTANT. It's not so bad, sir.

THE CLERK. All my life I've wanted to own Texas and Mary Smith.

THE ACCOUNTANT. I'm sorry, sir.

THE CLERK. I've always wanted to throw money away.

THE ACCOUNTANT. I know how you feel, sir. Why, sometimes I pretend I'm rich and I give a bootblack a dime instead of a nickel and I feel great for weeks.

THE CLERK. All my life I've dreamed about Texas.

(The telephone rings. The ACCOUNTANT *listens; hangs up.)*

THE ACCOUNTANT. I hate to tell you, sir, but it looks very bad. A messenger is on his way over with your balance. All your properties have been attached to cover losses.

THE CLERK. All the land and all the automobiles and all the fine apartment houses and all the toys?

THE ACCOUNTANT. Yes, sir, all the clothes, too. Now you have nothing but the clothes you are wearing and what's inside them.

THE CLERK. Have you any idea how much my balance will be?

THE ACCOUNTAN. I have an idea it will be very little, sir.

THE CLERK. I haven't had a decent meal in twenty days. I've been too excited to eat. When I was a clerk I used to get real hungry and eat like a horse. I used to eat anything. Now I don't even *want* to eat.

THE ACCOUNTANT. I hope there's enough for a good hearty twenty-five-cent dinner, sir.

THE CLERK. Thanks, Smith.

(The Postal Telegraph MESSENGER *arrives. The* CLERK *signs.)*

MESSENGER. This envelope contains your full balance, sir.

THE CLERK. Thanks.

(The CLERK *tears open the envelope, a nickel drops to the floor, he picks up the coin, and is about to go away. He remembers the harmonica in his hand.)*

THE CLERK. *(To the* PEDDLER*)* I'm sorry. I'll have to give you back your harmonica. I have no money. All my life I've wanted a harmonica.

THE PEDDLER. That's all right. Keep it. One is enough. You don't need a dozen. Just one. It's like singing.

THE CLERK. I'll remember your kindness.

The Old Refrain again.

And back to the subway.

SUBWAY CIRCUS

9

THE IMMORTALS

The Dreamer: A CORPORAL *of the Salvation Army.*

Others: A DRUNKARD. A WHORE. A STUDENT. A *sandwich* MAN *named* GOD. *Several* CRIPPLES.

THE SCENE: *A street corner. On the back-drop is painted a portion of the city and something that should suggest religious infinity, limitlessness: the holy universe, endless, without beginning and without end.*

When the SANDWICH MAN *stares at the* CORPORAL, *this part of the back-drop is to become glowing red, like fire.*

This is dreamed, of course, by the weary CORPORAL *of the Salvation Army.*

He is standing in the street with a big drum which he beats every once in a while.

A CRIPPLE *on crutches crosses the stage, paying no attention to the* CORPORAL.

The CORPORAL *speaks to the* DRUNKARD *and the* WHORE.

THE CORPORAL. Turn away, brother. Turn away from the evils of the world, sister. Lift your heart to God and be born again. Be as a child again. Turn now, before it is too late, brother. Do not drown in sin, sister. God is an angry God. *(Boom on the drum.)* His wrath can destroy the whole world in the twinkling of an eye. He will send fire and flood through the world and all who are evil will burn and drown while the pure in heart will be saved.

(A MAN with no legs who rolls about on a platform resting on roller skates rolls across the stage.)

THE WHORE. The pure in heart? What do you know about the heart?

THE CORPORAL. You must be ready for the wrath of God, brother. You must be ready to leave your mortal flesh and die. Are you ready, brother?

THE DRUNKARD. Yes, and the sooner the better.

THE CORPORAL. No, brother, you are not ready to die.

THE DRUNKARD. Listen, Sargeant, don't tell *me* I'm not ready to die when I tell you I *am* ready to die. Who are you, anyway? My name is John Smith and I'm thirty-seven years old and I'm ready to die, any day. Don't tell me I'm not ready to die. *(To the WHORE)* He says I'm not ready to die. This little punk telling *me* I'm not ready to die.

THE WHORE. You'll live to be a hundred. You'll die a million times before they put you into the ground, and you'll live longer than the ones who eat to live and pray to live and spend all their time worrying about microbes.

THE DRUNKARD. I got a sister in San Francisco. My mother's dead.

THE WHORE. I know all about it. You don't have to tell me.

THE CORPORAL. There is no time to lose, for it is written that God is an angry God and his wrath will destroy a sinful world.

THE DRUNKARD. That's fine. That suits me fine. How soon do you expect it to happen? I'm all jittery, waiting.

THE CORPORAL. When the world wallows in sin, God will destroy the world.

THE WHORE. It's been wallowing a long, long time. As far back as I can remember.

THE DRUNKARD. I guess I've done my share of wallowing, but I'll do some more if you say the word. Listen, pal, if you're sure just a little more wallowing will do the trick, I'll go out and wallow all through the city. I'm one of the best wallowers in the United States.

(A YOUNG MAN *joins the audience: he is a college boy, a student.)*

THE STUDENT. Karl Marx says religion is the opium of the people.

THE WHORE. This isn't religion, you dope. Not what he *says,* anyway. Maybe what he *means.* And what if it is the opium of the people? Do you think the people don't need opium?

THE STUDENT. It's a trick they have to keep the people satisfied. When they are hungry they pray instead of *demanding* food.

THE CORPORAL. I tell you, you must turn away and be as children again. You must not wait until the last minute.

(A SANDWICH MAN *appears. The sign advertises a full meal for ten cents.)*

THE SANDWICH MAN. I am God.

THE DRUNKARD. *(Shakes his hand)* I'm delighted to make your acquaintance. I've heard a lot about you.

THE SANDWICH MAN. I can look at a man and make him die.

THE DRUNKARD. All right, look at me. Are you looking?

THE SANDWICH MAN. I don't want *you* to die.

THE DRUNKARD. Listen, pal, you wouldn't go back on a pal, would you?

THE SANDWICH MAN. I want *you* to live.

THE DRUNKARD. You're a hell of a God.

THE STUDENT. *(To the* WHORE*)* You see? That's what Capitalism does to people.

THE WHORE. Don't be so wise. Don't be so sure it's Capitalism.

THE STUDENT. It is, though.

THE DRUNKARD. *(To the* SANDWICH MAN*)* Make *him* die, pal. Let's see you make *him* die. He says he's ready to die. Go ahead, pal, look at *him* and make *him* die. *(He points to the* CORPORAL.*)*

THE SANDWICH MAN. I *want* him to die. *(He stares at the* CORPORAL. *The* CORPORAL *trembles. There is a roar of thunder. Quotations from the Bible in a deep voice that speaks with finality. The* DRUNKARD, *the* WHORE, *and the* STUDENT *go away. The* CORPORAL *begins to sink to his knees. The* SANDWICH MAN *goes away. The* CORPORAL *turns and runs. The subway roars. The turnstile appears. The* CORPORAL *drops a nickel.)*

And back to the subway again.

SUBWAY CIRCUS

10

THE MORNING SONG

The Dreamer: An ITALIAN FRUIT PEDDLER.

THE SCENE: *An empty world. A world beginning. Morning. The new day. The beginning of fresh life. An endless road.*

The Event: The PEDDLER *enters this world when it is dark and silent.*

He stares at the scene, admiring it, and then says a few words in Italian.

Very slowly the scene accepts light, as the world accepts the light of the sun each morning.

The ITALIAN *speaks very quietly at first, then more boldly as the light increases. Then, as the light increases, he begins to hum, then sing softly to himself: only fragments.*

Gradually the sun begins to rise.

The ITALIAN *begins to sing in earnest.*

The song is: O Sole Mio.

His only accompaniment is a violin and an accordion.

*When the song ends the Scene is flooded with light.
It is day in the world, Monday or Tuesday.*

And back to the subway for the last time.

The play ends.

This play is an American play. It is a play which seeks to suggest some of the potentialities of our theatre. The play needs good American painters for the back-drops, which should be works of art, as wall paintings, frescoes and murals, are works of art. It needs good American composers. It needs people who are interested in the art of the theatre; the art of acting; the art of dancing; the art of light and color on the stage. It is my feeling that such people are numerous in America, and that many of them are idle. Needlessly idle. I feel that this play may very well serve the purpose of bringing these people together and putting their various talents to work. I believe I should point out that the brevity of the play may be misleading—may give the impression that there is little to work with. I suggest a careful examination of each episode.

One of the objects of the play is to bring together effectively the various arts and crafts related to the theatre, but not often utilized by the theatre. I feel confident that the result will be a work of delight to the beholder, and a work of some importance to the American theatre.

THE OFFICE PLAYS
Two full length plays by Adam Bock

THE RECEPTIONIST
Comedy / 2m, 2f / Interior
At the start of a typical day in the Northeast Office, Beverly
deals effortlessly with ringing phones and her colleague's ro-
mantic troubles. But the appearance of a charming rep from
the Central Office disrupts the friendly routine. And as the
true nature of the company's business becomes apparent,
The Receptionist raises disquieting, provocative questions
about the consequences of complicity with evil.

"...Mr. Bock's poisoned Post-it note of a play."
- New York Times

"Bock's intense initial focus on the routine goes to the heart of
The Receptionist's pointed, painfully timely allegory... elliptical,
provocative play..."
- Time Out New York

THE THUGS
Comedy / 2m, 6f / Interior
The Obie Award winning dark comedy about work, thunder and
the mysterious things that are happening on the 9th floor of a big
law firm. When a group of temps try to discover the secrets that
lurk in the hidden crevices of their workplace, they realize they
would rather believe in gossip and rumors than face dangerous
realities.

"Bock starts you off giggling, but leaves you with a chill."
- Time Out New York

"... a delightfully paranoid little nightmare that is both more
chillingly realistic and pointedly absurd than anything
John Grisham ever dreamed up."
- New York Times

SAMUELFRENCH.COM

CPSIA information can be obtained
at www.ICGtesting.com
Printed in the USA
LVOW10s0307220517
535380LV00007B/236/P